TO

_____

FROM

_____

ON

_____

365 WAYS TO DATE YOUR LOVE

A DAILY GUIDE TO CREATIVE ROMANCE

365 WAYS TO DATE YOUR LOVE
A DAILY GUIDE TO CREATIVE ROMANCE

BY TOMIMA EDMARK

THE SUMMIT PUBLISHING GROUP ~ FORT WORTH. TEXAS

THE SUMMIT PUBLISHING GROUP
2000 E. Lamar Blvd., Suite 600, Arlington, Texas 76006

00 01 02 03   6   7   8   9   10

Library of Congress Cataloging-in-Publication Data

Edmark, Tomima
365 ways to date your love: a daily guide to creative romance /
by Tomima Edmark.
p. cm.

ISBN 1-56530-174-9

1. Dating (Social customs)—Miscellanea. I. Title.

HQ801.E35 1995
646.7'7—dc20   95-31439
                                        CIP

✦ DEDICATION ✦

This book is dedicated to the man who makes
every date a dream come true:
my husband, Stephen.
I love you, darling!

✦ INTRODUCTION ✦

It's happened to everyone. The phone rings. You answer it. After a short exchange of pleasantries, the person on the other end bumbles out, "Would you like to go out with me Friday night?" Quickly, you call up your daytimer on your memory screen, scan your Friday plans, find nothing, and respond with, "Sure." They then counter with the all-too-common stymied response of, "Great! So what do you want to do?" Well, what DO you do?

Basically, you have two choices: one, return the volley with, "Oh, I don't care. Whatever you want," and risk spending the evening watching airplanes land; or two, run a mental brain sort on local restaurants until you find one you're not completely bored with to suggest. Wouldn't it be great if you always had a great, fun, and unique suggestion for a date? Well, since you're reading this, you do!

365 Ways to Date Your Love is a collection of great suggestions for spending time with someone you care about. A date,

7

in general terms, is "an appointment between two persons of the opposite sex for pleasant companionship during a specified time." O.K., but then an appointment with your hairstylist or personal trainer qualifies, too. What makes the dates in this book special is that they're designed to enhance the relationship. You won't find any standard fare restaurant/movie dates. Instead, you'll find unusual, silly, and romantic dates designed to nurture emotions and companionship.

Dates, like almost everything in life, should have variety. However, there is a kind of dating etiquette that should never change if you want the date to be a success.

- ✤ Dress accordingly. You don't want the other person to be embarrassed by the way you look.
- ✤ Consider the finances of the person paying. Don't put them in the awkward position of not having enough money to cover the date.
- ✤ Choose a place that's quiet. Going to a noisy spot makes communication difficult.
- ✤ End the date after a reasonable time. The end of a date should leave both parties looking forward to the next time instead of sighing with relief that it's finally over.
- ✤ Thank the person paying for the evening. A date should

not end with one of you feeling taken advantage of or not appreciated.

This book is a perfect gift for any single person or married couple you know. For that matter, it's perfect for you or your spouse. Let's face it, everyone has a dry spell when it comes to thinking of a fun date every once in a while. So keep this book around as a reference when those times come, and you'll never have to drag yourself through a boring date again.

✦ 1 ✦

JUST DESSERTS

Find out (on the sly) the restaurant that serves
your Love's favorite dessert. Make a reservation,
order two desserts, and enjoy the evening.

✦ 2 ✦

ADMISSION FOR TWO

It can be a movie, sporting, cultural or musical event. The
key is it's something your Love has always wanted to attend,
but you've never been crazy about.

✦ 3 ✦

MAP IT OUT

Find a map of your city or a place close to your home.
Together, select an area the two of you have never seen. Now,
set out on a driving adventure to the site.

❖ 4 ❖

PAIR OF BOOKENDS

Sit back-to-back with your Love on the floor,
bed, or couch. Begin sharing your hopes and fears
while your Love listens. When you're done
it's your partner's turn. Afterward, discuss with your Love
what's been said, but don't change your sitting positions.

❖ 5 ❖

SPRINKLE, SPRINKLE

Turn on your sprinkler or find some already on.
Have fun running through them together.

❖ 6 ❖

JAVA

The two of you go in search of the best coffee
in your area. Ask for samples. If there are no samples,
share one cup in each location.

✦ 7 ✦

YOU, ME. ME, YOU.

Switch roles for the evening. Warning: Don't take this as an opportunity to point out all your partner's faults.

✦ 8 ✦

RISKY BUSINESS

Spend the evening slow dancing in your underwear... in private, of course.

✦ 9 ✦

PIG-OUT

Agree to blow your diet. Go to a store or restaurant and buy or order everything you've been craving lately.

✦ 10 ✦

NEWLYWED

Drive around with a "Just Married" sign on the back of your car. Enjoy the reactions.

✦ 11 ✦

LEAPFROG

When was the last time you played leapfrog together? For
that matter, has there ever been a first time?

✦ 12 ✦

DREAM HOUSE

Drive around with your Love to find your future dream house.
It doesn't matter if you can't afford it...it's a dream.

✦ 13 ✦

DRIVE-THRU

Rate the drive-thru fast-food windows in your area.
See how many toys you can collect.

✦ 14 ✦

STEP IN STYLE

Gather up all the shoes the two of you need repaired or
shined and go get them fixed.

❖ 15 ❖

SEA CRUISE

This cruise is done without a boat.
Find a body of water—be it a tub, pool, or puddle—
and settle in for an afternoon on the deck.

❖ 16 ❖

PUPPY LOVE

Find a friend with a puppy and ask if the two of you can
puppy-sit for the afternoon. Or, shop pet stores asking,
"How much is that doggy in the window?"

❖ 17 ❖

USE YOUR HEAD

Practice balancing a book on your head.
Then, compete with each other to see who can take off the
most pieces of clothing before the book falls.

✦ 18 ✦

BAR NONE
Go shopping for the best bar of soap, bar none.

✦ 19 ✦

LOTTO
Buy Lotto tickets for every state you can.
Then, watch for the results.

✦ 20 ✦

LEIBOWITZ WANT-TO-BE
Spend the day taking pictures of each other. Let strangers take pictures of the two of you. Drop them off at a one-hour photo processor and go have coffee until they're ready.

✦ 21 ✦

TAFFY
Make taffy together. Have fun pulling it until it's ready.

❖ 22 ❖

ZOO REVIEW

Decide which animal most reminds you of you and which
animal reminds you of your Love and write it down. Share
the results and have a fun spirited debate over the selections.

❖ 23 ❖

MYSTERY FOOD

Find a restaurant with unusual or foreign dishes
on the menu. Agree to order only those dishes you don't
understand or recognize. Have fun guessing
and tasting the foods.

❖ 24 ❖

PEOPLE & PLACES

Find a spot to sit in a "high traffic" public place
like a mall, airport, or hotel lobby. Guess the passersby's
occupations, ages, and type of pets they own.

✦ 25 ✦

GENE KELLY WANNA BE'S

Take his cue from *Singing in the Rain* and do it the next time
it rains. Puddle splash each other, let cars splash you, and
generally get soaked the funniest way possible.
Afterward, help each other dry off.

✦ 26 ✦

LEMONADE STAND

Kids do it, why not you? Spend the afternoon
selling lemonade in your neighborhood. You'll meet your
neighbors as well as have fun. Advertise all proceeds
go to a local charity.

✦ 27✦

NEWSWORTHY

Visit your local library together and look up each other's
birthday in as many newspapers as you can find. Make copies
of notable articles and put them in a notebook as a keepsake.

✦ 28 ✦

UP ON THE ROOF
Find a roof to climb onto some evening. Bring a blanket,
music, beverage of choice, and stargaze together.

✦ 29 ✦

PROM NIGHT
Find out where a local high school is having its prom.
Position yourselfs discretely near the front door and enjoy
watching the seniors arrive.

✦ 30 ✦

SHARE & SHARE ALIKE
All food ordered must be shared
with each other. Each can have their own silverware,
but only one dish can be brought at a time.

✦ 31 ✦

FLEAS & OLD TIRES
Spend the day shopping flea markets or garage sales
looking for bargain treasure.

✦ 32 ✦

PHONE FUN
Locate two pay phones in view of each other. Call the other
phone until some passerby picks up. When one answers, ask
the person a question. The right answer has an award of
twenty-five cents which can be found in the coin return.

✦ 33 ✦

BEND & BAG
Near your home, find a spot that could use some
cleaning up. One of you holds the bag, while the other one
bends to pick up the litter. When one gets tired, switch
duties. This date could be contagious.

❖ 34 ❖

FLOP, FLOP, PLOP

Find a pond or other calm water where the two of you can skip rocks. See who can skip the most times. Challenge each other to skip non-traditional shaped rocks.

❖ 35 ❖

FIELD OF DREAMS

Find a field. Bring a boom box, food, beverage, and blanket. Eat, drink, sleep and slow dance.

❖ 36 ❖

IN THE CLOUDS

The two of you lie outside on your backs and search for objects in the clouds. Make it more interesting by alternating your direction and by changing positions with your Love.

✦ 37 ✦

RECESS

Find a playground where the two of you can swing,
ride a merry-go-round, seesaw, and play on a jungle gym.
Afterward, eat a snack and take a nap.

✦ 38 ✦

INCOGNITO

Michael Jackson does it. Why not the two of you?
Visit thrift stores together to come up with your disguise.
Stroll the neighborhood to see if anyone recognizes you.
Some fun accessories include hats, glasses,
canes, jewelry, wigs, and purses.

✦ 39 ✦

NEIGHBORHOOD BIKERS

On a pair of bikes, go slowly down every street together.
You'd be surprised what you've never noticed before.

+ 40 +

THAT SPECIAL FIRST TIME

Remember that special first time you shared your love with
each other? See if you can recreate the moment.

+ 41 +

FINDING FAME

Think of someone in your area who's famous. It could be a
politician, movie star or socialite. Spend the day trying to
catch a glimpse—maybe even an autograph.

+ 42 +

HONEY, BUNNY

Discuss which name of affection you'd like your
Love to call you, e.g. Honey, Handsome, Snookims. Now,
together create a signal to be used in public to mean "I Love
You," e.g. double-hand squeeze, wink, a jig. Go for a walk or
out to dinner, and practice using both.

✦ 43 ✦

SWINGIN'

Locate a swing. Trade-off pushing each other. Porch swings
also work for this date, but you both have to push.

✦ 44 ✦

IMPOSTORS

Decide what two famous people you both look like. Make a
reservation in their names. Arrive looking as much like them
as possible. Enjoy the reactions. Try not to break character.

✦ 45 ✦

LACE-UPS

Give a lift to you and your Love's lace-up shoes.
Together, go on a shoelace shopping spree.
Consider ribbons or laces as an option.

❖ 46 ❖

FOUR TOPS

Each of you picks four favorite songs. Alternate lip-synching in front of your Love. Include choreography, and don't forget that makeshift microphone (try a hairbrush or remote controller).

❖ 47 ❖

SUPER SNOOP

Always wondered where people you know or work with live? Make a list, find their address, grab a map, and go snoop. You may want to wear a disguise.

❖ 48 ❖

WADING AROUND

Find a fountain, baby pool, ocean, stream, whatever. Take off your shoes and socks, roll up your pants or hike up your skirt, and go wade.

❖ 49 ❖

TEMPTATION

Take this dare: Place two of your favorite cookies
on a plate in full view. Now, the two of you spend one hour
in the cookies' company. Either help each other
to resist or tempt each other to indulge. After the hour is up,
go eat them. Have milk on hand.

❖ 50 ❖

SPIT IT OUT

Together, learn to become expert spitters. Practice
different scenarios—out the window of a moving car, while
running, during baseball, over your left shoulder.

❖ 51 ❖

SHOWER POWER

At night, or during the day when
no one is looking, take a shower outside together.
Bring soap, buckets of warm water, and towels.

✦ 52 ✦

COURTROOM DRAMA

In earlier days, entertainment was found in the local courthouse watching trials. O. J. seems to have revived the trend.
Spend an afternoon in the courthouse nearest you.

✦ 53 ✦

MOVING PARTS

Do you know how to wiggle your nose? Ears? Nostrils? Scalp?
Does your partner? Have fun teaching each other what you
know about this subject.

✦ 54 ✦

I SPY

Acknowledge having a birth mark, a certain scar, a mole
shaped like a carrot, etc., and allow your Love thirty seconds
to find it on your body. If not found, show and tell.
Now, have your Love do the same. Continue until
all imperfections are identified.

+ 55 +

PAJAMA PARTY
Dress in comfortable bedclothes. Now, get into bed,
have dinner, and read or watch a movie.

+ 56 +

SPAGHETTI DINNER
It's simple, delicious, and fun to eat. Put the spaghetti in one
big bowl between the two of you. Grab two forks and let the
fun begin. Note: Spaghetti is also good cold the next day.

+ 57 +

CHOP, CHOP, CHOPSTICKS
Have a breakfast of eggs, bacon, cereal, and toast—
eating with only chopsticks.

✦ 58 ✦

HAIR DO DEUX

Make an appointment for the two of you to get your
haircut at the same time and place.

✦ 59 ✦

A CLEAN DUET

In the shower (you don't have to actually
be taking one), sing a duet with your Love. You'll be
surprised how good you think you sound.

✦ 60 ✦

WISH HUNT

Make a list of all the things you can think of to wish on and
then go on a wish hunt. Look for things like: a first star, a
four-leaf clover, a white horse, a new moon, a car with only
one working headlight, and a coin for a fountain.

✦ 61 ✦

RELATIONSHIP VOWS

You and your Love sit down and talk about
what declarations or promises you want to make to each
other on behalf of the relationship. When you both agree,
write them down. If you're already married, update your vows
and read them on your next anniversary.

✦ 62 ✦

HELLO INTERNET

If the two of you don't know about it, it's time you did.
Take a class together on the worldwide Internet to see what
new opportunities are waiting for you.

✦ 63 ✦

FROM THE VINE

Take a wine tasting class together.
Find out which wines you both like and dislike.

✦ 64 ✦

STAR LIGHT, STAR BRIGHT
On a beautiful, clear night lie outside in the buff
on a blanket with your Love. Watch for shooting stars.

✦ 65 ✦

BEDTIME STORY
The two of you create your own romantic tale. Begin with a
steamy introduction, then take turns embellishing the story.

✦ 66 ✦

GROWING WILD
Find a place where wild flowers grow,
and the two of you go collecting.

✦ 67 ✦

DREAM DATE
Over dinner, share your dreams, aspirations,
and goals in life with each other.

✦ 68 ✦

SETTING SUN

Locate the optimal sunset-viewing spot in your area. Make
a date to watch it together. Perhaps, bring a picnic dinner.
Don't forget a blanket to sit on or wrap around each other.

✦ 69 ✦

DRIVE-IN

If you can find a drive-in movie, go. If not, improvise. Take
your TV and VCR and place it on the hood of your car. The
two of you sit in your car and watch a rented movie while
nibbling on popcorn, hot dogs, and necks.

✦ 70 ✦

TRUE LIFE LIMERICK

Remember the limerick: "Love and marriage go
together like a horse and carriage"? Well, take this limerick
literally and go for a ride in a horse-drawn carriage
with your Love. You each must sing at least one chorus of this
limerick—while in the carriage.

+ 71 +

DOWN UNDER

Head to the nearest shopping mall. Each of you
has one hour to find the craziest underwear for the other.
One hour later, reunite and "show and tell" by
either taking your Love to the store or by buying the
underwear for a private showing.

+ 72 +

ROYAL FLUSH

Each of you pick a different color of bathroom tissue and
place one square on the surface of the water. Flush. The last
one's square down the tube wins a point. Play to fifteen.

+ 73 +

DOLLAR BILL

Have a contest to see how many different shapes can
be created by folding a dollar bill.

❧ 74 ❧

CONTRABAND

Devise a plan for how the two of you are going to
get your own snack food into a movie theater without being
detected. Execute your plan.

❧ 75 ❧

SPELLING BEE

Conduct one with your Love. Each pick words for the other.
A definition and origin may be given if asked.

❧ 76 ❧

TREASURE HUNT

Set out together for a walk to find a beautiful rock, shell, or
piece of wood. Start a collection of walking memories. Bring
back walking memories from vacations.

✦ 77 ✦

DECK THE HALLS
Collect decorations for the next holiday and decorate your
home(s) in the holiday spirit.

✦ 78 ✦

BABY-SITTER
The two of you surprise someone who has a baby
by offering to baby-sit.

✦ 79 ✦

BETWEEN THE SHEETS
Wrap each other in sheets to look like Romans. Now, when
in Rome, do as the Romans do!

✦ 80 ✦

KIDNAP
Have a friend kidnap and then deliver your Love to you at a
special spot. As a bonus, serve your Love's favorite meal.

✦ 81 ✦

BULL'S EYE
Find a bar with dartboards and play darts with your Love.

✦ 82 ✦

THE"G-O-O"
Tune into the "Grand Ole Opry" and sit and
listen to it together.

✦ 83 ✦

HE SAID, SHE SAID
You and your Love alternate telling each other the many
things you love most about each other.

✦ 84 ✦

FORGET-ME-NOT
Over a bowl of popcorn, try to
remember as many past dates with your Love as possible.
See if you can agree on what each was wearing.

✦ 85 ✦
THEATER FOR TWO
Select a play you both like. Find a secluded
spot outside or inside and reenact it with your Love.
Hint: Choose one with a love scene.

✦ 86 ✦
RELATIVE NAMES
Before the next family function, the two of you
agree on code names for the family members. e.g.: "The
clock" is Grandfather, "Tomato soup" is Aunt Betty.
Now you can speak in code at the next family function. For
instance, "Darling, look at the clock."

✦ 87 ✦
STRANGER IN NEED
Call the local hospital's cancer ward and ask if a particular
patient could use a friendly visit from a pair of strangers bear-
ing gifts. The gifts could be magazines, plants, etc.

✦ 88 ✦

ONE-TWO-THREE

Find a pair of tricycles and have a race with your Love.
Or, just wheel around the neighborhood together.

✦ 89 ✦

TRAIL BLAZING

Find an offbeat restaurant the two of you have never gone to
and try a new dining experience.

✦ 90 ✦

ULTIMATE FOOTSIE

Massage your Love's feet, and your Love
will follow you anywhere.

✦ 91 ✦

COUCH SHOPPING

Tune into one or several of the home shopping channels on
TV together. Call and try to get your voices on the air.

✦ 92 ✦

COME HOME
Go to one of your high school's homecoming games together.
Compare the way it is today to the way it once was.

✦ 93 ✦

FOR THE BIRDS
During the winter, go on a walk together
scattering birdseed for the birds to collect.

✦ 94 ✦

TALK SHOWS
Tune into talk shows with the volume off
and try to guess the show's topic.

✦ 95 ✦

READ THE LABELS
Take on the project of labeling all the VCR and cassette
tapes you both have laying around.

✦ 96 ✦

CITY'S FINEST

Call your local police station and find out who
the policemen are that are assigned to your neighborhood.
Together, go meet them and learn about
your neighborhood. If this was fun, do the same
with the fire department.

✦ 97 ✦

ANIMAL KINGDOM

Go out to dinner together. What animals do
your waiter and the people around you remind you of most?
You must agree on the animal.

✦ 98 ✦

SURPRISE MAIL

Watch a shopping channel or thumb through
mail-order catalogs until the two of you find something you
are sure would make someone you know laugh.
Send it to them anonymously.

❧ 99 ❧

SOMEONE ELSE'S TREASURE

Go through your house together and gather up all the
things you no longer need or use. Deliver them to a homeless
shelter, needy family, or charity. This date feels great.

❧ 100 ❧

LOCAL ATTRACTION

What famous monument, garden, gallery, or local attraction
have you never taken the time to visit because you think it's
always going to be there? Well, visit it now with your Love.

❧ 101 ❧

FACES & PLACES

With a camera in hand, spend the day together asking people
if they'll let you photograph them making their funniest face.
This could be the start of a great collection.

✦ 102 ✦

SAY "CHEESE"

The two of you take a Polaroid camera to a public spot.
Offer to take passersby's pictures and then give it to them.

✦ 103 ✦

FREE DELIVERY

Go on an early morning walk together in your neighborhood.
For those neighbors who have the paper delivered, take the
paper and place it on their porch as a morning surprise. If it's
a rainy morning, they'll appreciate it even more.

✦ 104 ✦

NEED FOR THE NEEDY

The two of you do the grocery shopping
for someone who is ill or elderly.

✦ 105 ✦

THE FLAMINGO

You need two squirt guns and clothing you
don't mind getting wet. Outside, each of you stand
on one foot—five feet apart. In one hand,
hold your squirt gun; in the other, hold one of your ankles
behind you. The goal is to maintain balance and
not let go of your foot. Ready, set, squirt!

✦ 106 ✦

PIE WISHING

Find a restaurant specializing in pies. You each
order a slice and watch how it's served to you. If the point is
served toward you, you get one wish. Now, cut off
the pie point and put it aside until the rest of the pie is eaten.
Finally, put the pie point in your mouth and make
a wish before swallowing. Turn your pie plate around three
times to ensure your wish comes true.

✦ 107 ✦

SNIFF TEST

Blindfold your Love to test his or her sense of smell. Spices
are fun, and so are colognes strategically placed on different
body parts. Now, reverse the roles to test your nose.

✦ 108 ✦

BECOME A LAWYER

You probably will, while playing the game of "Life"
with your Love for the evening.

✦ 109 ✦

BATH PHOTOGRAPH

Photograph your love (with your Love's consent)
taking a bath. If you don't like your bathtub, rent a room for
the night. Be sure to have plenty of bubbles.
Nude shots are a no-no. Go for a shot that is suitable to
frame and hang in your bathroom.

❖ 110 ❖
HUNTING FOR GREEN
Head for an unmown lawn or field.
Search together until you find a four-leaf clover.

❖ 111 ❖
MEMORY LANE
Drive your Love to your old neighborhood and
take them on a tour of your youth. Include schools, friend's
houses, the place you received your first kiss,
and local hangouts. If possible, have your Love take you on a
tour of his or her neighborhood, the next night.

❖ 112 ❖
ON YOUR MARKS, GET SET, DRESS
Set your Love's clothes on the bed, turn out the lights, and
time how long it takes them to get dressed. Then it's your turn.
You can be naughty and turn the clothes inside out. Penalty
points are added to the time for each item missed or worn
inside out. Be sure to check that underwear was put on right.

❖ 113 ❖

CATCH A FALLING LEAF

This is no mean feat, especially in a breeze. Superstition says catch twelve leaves and you'll have a year's good luck.

❖ 114 ❖

GET OUT THE VOTE

Spend the day together researching candidates and issues that will be voted on in the next election.

❖ 115 ❖

JUGGLING

Do you two know how to juggle? Have fun learning together. Find three balls and a juggler or buy a book.

❖ 116 ❖

BY THE LIGHT OF THE MOON

During the next full moon, play soft romantic music and dance cheek-to-cheek under the moonlight.

✤ 117 ✤

BOJANGLES

If the two of you were to panhandle, what would be
your calling? Singing? Dancing? Well find a corner,
throw down a hat, and test your skills.

✤ 118 ✤

CUT UP

You'll need two pairs of scissors and lots
of paper. Have fun making snowflakes, paper dolls, or doilies.
Save them to decorate your windows later.

✤ 119 ✤

CRIME FIGHTERS

Together, research your home(s) to determine what types of
security devices you need for protection.
Then, buy and install them.

✦ 120 ✦

YOGA

No, you don't have to become a human pretzel.
Yoga is great. Find a class nearby that you can both join.

✦ 121 ✦

BUFFORAMA

Share an evening of nudity.

✦ 122 ✦

LIGHTS OUT

Share the day's experiences with your Love in
the dark. Listening only gives new insights, images, and focus.

✦ 123 ✦

CELLULITE RUB

Research has shown that massaging the buttocks
with oil reduces cellulite. Whether it works or not,
this is a must try with your Love.

✦ 124 ✦

THE HOUSE THAT DOYLE BUILT
Don't just talk about a house of cards.
Make one together. See how big of one you can make,
then have fun blowing it down.

✦ 125 ✦

I DO REDO
Recreate your wedding. Buy a small wedding cake, recreate
the reception menu, get out the VCR and photos, find your
"first dance" music, and throw rice on or at each other.

✦ 126 ✦

SUNDAY MORNING
Don't bolt out of bed this Sunday. Rather,
stay in bed until noon with your Love. Read the paper, have
breakfast, play backgammon, or....

✦ 127 ✦

BERRY PICKIN'

Find a neighborhood berry patch or go to a farm
that let's you pick berries. When you get home, make them
into jam, juice, or eat them plain.

✦ 128 ✦

FLY PAPER

Make paper airplanes together, then have a
paper dogfight with them.

✦ 129 ✦

COOKIE MACHINE

Get out the aprons and grease up the cookie sheets for a
marathon cookie bake with your Love. Give the cookies to
co-workers, neighbors, friends in the hospital, the garbage
man, the mailman, or just eat them yourselves.

✦ 130 ✦

HIDDEN TREASURE CHESTS
Explore the creases in your couches, under the pillows
of your chairs, in the pockets of your clothes, and the drawers
where you throw change. Meet back together
and count up your booty. Depending on the amount,
go to a movie, dinner, or Laundromat.

✦ 131 ✦

SKATE DATE
Choose roller, ice or in-line skates
and have some fun. Don't forget padding.

✦ 132 ✦

HIRED HELP
Dress up as a French maid and an English butler
and agree to wait on each other.

❖ 133 ❖

FEET FETISH

Plan an evening devoted to each other's feet. Begin with
both dressing in robes. Next, have two tubs with warm soapy
water for soaking with fluffy towels near by for drying off.
Now, sitting across from each other, each put one foot in the
other's lap and begin pedicuring or massaging the other's foot.
Then, switch and do the same with the other foot.

❖ 134 ❖

BOXIN'

Together shop for lunch pails for each of you.
When you get home fill them with each other's favorite
foods, and take them to work for lunch tomorrow.

❖ 135 ❖

DON'T WALK

Don't just walk on your next walk,
put some skipping into it as well.

❖ 136 ❖

IT'S IN THE NAME

Go around your home together giving names
to your electrical inanimate objects, e.g.: TV = Tommy
Tuner, VCR = Midnight Flasher, Alarm Clock = Screamin'
Mimi, Computer = Big Brother. Now, try and use these
names for the next couple of days.

❖ 137 ❖

SIGN ON

Take a class together on sign language. So you
don't know anyone who's deaf? It doesn't matter,
simply use it on your Love.

❖ 138 ❖

THE REAL MEANING

Each grab a dictionary and try to stump the other with
words the other one doesn't know. Keep a list. Next morning,
see if the two of you can remember what they mean.

✦ 139 ✦

HOT DOG

Have a weenie roast for dinner. Start a fire
in the fireplace or improvise with your stovetop. Use sticks to
skewer your weenies and don't forget the potato salad.

✦ 140 ✦

PAY PHONE PICKUP

Find two pay phones. Now call your Love,
as if for the first time, and try to get him or her to go
out with you on a date. Flatter them,
use pickup lines, ask them their sign—just have fun.

✦ 141 ✦

HANDY WORK

Sit between a wall and lamp and see
how many silhouette animals you can make.
If you're really into it, stage a production.

+ 142 +

SOME ASSEMBLY REQUIRED
Buy that item you've always wanted, but
didn't want to assemble, and the two of you spend
the day putting it together.

+ 143 +

HAT, CAP, BONNET
Spend the day searching for the
perfect millinery choice for each of you.

+ 144 +

INDOORS GOES OUTDOORS
Haul some of your indoor furniture outdoors
for the evening. Not just a chair or two, but significant
pieces like the sofa, television, dining room table,
or even your entire bedroom.

✦ 145 ✦

HOT SHOTS

Sit down together and finally organize all those photographs
that have been laying around your home.

✦ 146 ✦

RESTROOM ADVENTURE

Think of the best ladies and men's rooms in your area.
Now devise a plan to let your Love see them.
You will need to check and make sure it's empty.
Stand guard as your Love checks it out.

✦ 147 ✦

RETURN DATE

Gather up all those things laying around your house
that need to be returned or exchanged. Spend the afternoon
taking care of them together. It goes faster if one can
stay in the car while the other runs in. Afterward, reward
your efforts with a great dessert or movie.

✦ 148 ✦

CONNECT THE DOTS

...or rather freckles and/or moles of your Love with a felt-tip water soluble pen. See what hidden shapes exist, then switch.

✦ 149 ✦

BREAKFAST PICNIC

Grab a picnic basket and set up breakfast under a tree some morning. Food suggestions include cereal, fruit, and muffins.

✦ 150 ✦

WALL PAINTING

Have a room that needs painting? Paint it together.

✦ 151 ✦

IT'S IN THE JEANS

Go on a shopping expedition looking
for the perfect pair of jeans for each of you.

✦ 152 ✦
GETTING PERSONAL
Collect all the personal ad sections you can find
from newspapers and magazines. Sit down together and over
coffee read them. Share personal favorites with your Love.

✦ 153 ✦
A DIRTY DATE
Break out from your usual character. The two of you
find a private place and talk dirty to each other. Say those
words you'd normally never say and invent
fantasies to shock your Love.

✦ 154 ✦
CLOSE SHAVE
Get out your razors and shave
each other. Trust and a steady hand are a must.

✦ 155 ✦

CULTURAL EVENT
Buy two tickets to a cultural event
you wouldn't usually go to, then go.

✦ 156 ✦

"HOW DO I LOVE THEE?"
Find a romantic poem book, then read the poems out loud to
each other. Share your interpretations with each other.

✦ 157 ✦

A PHONE CALL AWAY
Pick up the phone and call each other's relatives to hear
childhood stories about each other.

✦ 158 ✦

REUNION
Together choose a friend, relative, or teacher you haven't
seen in a long time and stage a reunion.

✦ 159 ✦

"ROW, ROW, ROW YOUR BOAT"

Borrow or rent a row boat and row around on a peaceful lake together. If you have a devilish side, splash or tip the boat over.

✦ 160 ✦

FOR YOUR AMUSEMENT

Spend the afternoon at an amusement park. Boldly go on rides you've never been on before.

✦ 161 ✦

NEED FOR SPEED

Rent a pair of dirt bikes or off-terrain vehicles and have fun chasing each other. Warning: you will get dirty.

✦ 162 ✦

LIFESTYLES

Share an evening over champagne wishes and caviar dreams.

❧ 163 ❧

TRIVIAL PURSUIT

On index cards, each privately write down fifteen
trivia questions about yourself and your relationship with
your Love. Now, take turns asking each other
the questions. The winner gets the sensual act of their
choice such as a kiss, massage, or....

❧ 164 ❧

MOVIE FIRST

Rent and watch the first movie you saw together.

❧ 165 ❧

RETURN TO HEAVEN

Recreate your honeymoon or your most
memorable vacation in your home. For instance, if you went
to Hawaii, wear leis and grass skirts, listen to Don Ho,
and sip piña coladas. If you bought souvenirs, bring them
out, oh, and don't forget the pictures.

✦ 166 ✦

TIME RELEASE

Make a time capsule of your relationship. Fill a box with
items symbolic of your personalities and life together. Perform
a ceremonious burial. Will it to someone or have your
children exhume it on a special anniversary.

✦ 167 ✦

ALMA MATER

Take your Love on a tour of your college or high school.
Point out special classrooms, your locker, the place where you
smoked your first cigarette or received your first kiss,
and any other special landmarks.

✦ 168 ✦

CONCERT FOR TWO

Rent a musician or singer to come
to your home for a private performance.

✦ 169 ✦

DECK THE HALLS
Make Christmas ornaments together, regardless
of the month. The ornaments could be gingerbread men,
painted plastic ornament balls, figures from clay, or anything.
Keep some and give the rest to friends and family.

✦ 170 ✦

A COUPLE OF COUPLES
Call that couple you've always wanted to double with and
spend an evening with them. If the time together was a disas-
ter, have fun talking to your Love about it afterward.

✦ 171 ✦

AMATEUR GLAMOUR
Each of you choose an outfit you'd like to see
your Love photographed wearing. Now, set up a makeshift
photographers studio in your home and click away.
Use lamps without their shades, find a wall for a backdrop,
and locate the best camera equipment possible.

✦ 172 ✦

IN THE SKIN

Find a spot for the two of you to go skinny dipping.
If the best you can find is a backyard and a hose, do it,
then streak the neighborhood, too.

✦ 173 ✦

HIGH TEA

Experience the tradition of the English high tea. Find a spot
near you that serves high tea; or read up on it, and the two of
you do it yourself. Usually, service is between 3:00-5:00 p.m.

✦ 174 ✦

UNITED WE STAND

Join or observe a protest march. Check the
news or call the police for the one nearest you.

✦ 175 ✦

MIDNIGHT SHOPPER

Many stores are now open twenty-four hours a day.
At midnight go shopping together. The grocery stores are
always quiet, and the produce is well stocked.

✦ 176 ✦

CARRY OUT

Call your Love's favorite restaurant and order
his or her favorite meal, but tell them you want it ready for
pickup. Pick up the food. Then, go together to
your Love's favorite picnic spot, and enjoy the meal.

✦ 177 ✦

EARLY BIRDS

Catch some worms and go fishin' before
the sun comes up. Have a great breakfast afterward.

✦ 178 ✦

WINDOW SHOPPING
Go window shopping together at night after the stores close.

✦ 179 ✦

UFO
Together, go to a place known for UFO sightings.
Spend the evening curled up on a blanket looking for
unidentified flying objects.

✦ 180 ✦

GO TO JAIL
You probably will, when you spend the evening playing
Monopoly with your Love.

✦ 181 ✦

LIFE AFTER DEATH .
Do you know what your Love thinks about it? Spend an afternoon discussing the subject.

✦ 182 ✦

COCKTAILS
Shake things up at a bartending class together.

✦ 183 ✦

COUCH POTATOES
Toe-to-toe on a sofa, each of you
silently read a book while playing footsie.

✦ 184 ✦

VACATION FANTASY
Discuss then research the ultimate vacation you'd want to
take together. Who knows, maybe you'll just go.
If not, agree to save until you can.

✦ 185 ✦

HOP ALONG
Together, jump rope for fun and fitness.
Jump to the rhymes you learned as children.

❖ 186 ❖

AGENT 007
Spy a spy store and go on surveillance.

❖ 187 ❖

FOR THE BIRDS
Build a distinctive birdhouse together.
Put it in a special place so the two of you can
enjoy watching your feathered friends.

❖ 188 ❖

THE PRICE IS RIGHT
Visit several pawnshops together and discover what your
material possessions are really worth.

❖ 189 ❖

HAPPY HOUR
Meet your Love after work at an elegant bar or restaurant
for a drink and conversation about the day's events.

✦ 190 ✦

PARADE OF HOMES
Spend Sunday afternoon touring
the parade of open houses in your town.

✦ 191 ✦

TRUCKIN'
People-watch while dining at a truck stop.

✦ 192 ✦

TO YOUR HEALTH
Spend time together having your
blood pressure and cholesterol levels checked.

✦ 193 ✦

STRANGER IN YOUR OWN KINGDOM
Get a tourist's perspective of your town
by going to the visitor's bureau. Guaranteed, you'll discover
something different to do around town.

✦ 194 ✦

PERSONAL DONATIONS

Go donate blood together. Make it more enjoyable
by bringing cookies and juice to have afterward. If you're
really feeling generous, reward the volunteers
who are taking the blood.

✦ 195 ✦

A 21-LETTER SALUTE

Locate a serviceman or woman who is overseas. Together,
write a letter or assemble a care package to send to them.

✦ 196 ✦

COOL SHADES

Spend the day searching for the ultimate
pair of sunglasses for each of you.

✦ 197 ✦

SOUND OFF
Schedule a Saturday afternoon together
to learn about all the different kinds of stereo equipment on
the market, and what it all does.

✦ 198 ✦

LOCAL SPORTS
Find the next Shaq, Bird, or Magic in your area
by attending a local basketball game. Watch the parents,
they're usually the most entertaining.

✦ 199 ✦

BY THE TAIL
Buy tickets for two to a sporting, cultural
or entertainment event. Have a candle lit tailgate party for
just the two of you, before the event.

✦ 200 ✦

JANE FONDA

Not! Rent one of the many exercise
videos available. Get in your workout clothes in front of the
TV and have fun together trying to follow the exercises.

✦ 201 ✦

I SCREAM. YOU SCREAM

Not for yogurt or ice milk, but the really
fattening stuff: ice cream. Make it together. The calories you
spend on the hand crank should burn off some of the extra
calories the two of you consume...well maybe.

✦ 202 ✦

TUBE FLOAT

On a lake, in a pool, or down a river,
enjoy floating along together on inner tubes.

✦ 203 ✦

CROQUET ANYONE?
Find a croquet set or devise a makeshift one
out of golf balls and paper tents. Enjoy the game outside
or in your living room.

✦ 204 ✦

WAR PAINT
Paint each other's face, then attend a concert,
sporting event, or new wave club.

✦ 205 ✦

RECORDING STUDIO
There are plenty of places that will make a recording
of the two of you singing to a soundtrack. Make a tape, then
take it home and listen to it. Depending on the results,
a ceremonious burning may be in order.

✦ 206 ✦

ANIMAL, VEGETABLE, OR MINERAL
Play charades together.

✦ 207 ✦

DEMOCRACY IN ACTION
Select a candidate or issue the two of you believe in and
together donate time working toward its success.

✦ 208 ✦

THE DOMINO EFFECT
Create your own effect by building a domino course together.
Flip to see who gets to set it off.

✦ 209 ✦

NET IT OUT
Buy a pair of butterfly nets and spend the day
catching butterflies.

✦ 210 ✦

GOING UP?
Elevator race to see who can get
to the top of the building first. Then, race going down.

✦ 211 ✦

TOUCH SENSITIVE
Learn the skill of Braille and then read together.

✦ 212 ✦

SELF-HELP
Collect all the self-help questionnaires
you can find in magazines. Both of you take the tests
separately, then compare results.

✦ 213 ✦

DOWN TO EARTH
Mix up or find some mud and have a
mud fight with each other. Then, go jump in the lake.

✦ 214 ✦

ARCADIAN
Video arcades are far from it! Spend a few hours
playing video games, then go lick your wounds
at a frozen yogurt store.

✦ 215 ✦

"CATALOG" SHOP?
No, catalog shop together. It's a great way
to find out what your Love might want
for an upcoming birthday or Christmas.

✦ 216 ✦

VH-1 & MTV
No, these are not multivitamins. They are
cable television channels. Find them on your TV and spend
a few hours watching, listening, and maybe
even dancing to them.

✦ 217 ✦

IT'S A HOBBY

Hobby shows are everywhere. Whether it's a
coin show, pet show, gun show, or baseball card show,
take your Love to one for the fun of it.

✦ 218 ✦

OPENING BID

Have fun attending an auction together.
Sign up for a bid number and join in the excitement.

✦ 219 ✦

CONTEST CONTESTANTS

Gather up all the contest forms
you can find in grocery stores, magazines, and in the mail.
Now, sit down, fill them out, and mail them.
Dream about what you will do with your winnings.

❖ 220 ❖

EARLY RISER
Wake your Love up early some
morning and go out for breakfast.

❖ 221 ❖

PERSONAL PIZZA
Create a pizza masterpiece together.

❖ 222 ❖

BRANCH OUT
Spend an afternoon climbing trees together. Bring a lunch.

❖ 223 ❖

ART CRITICS
Browse art galleries together
and critique (not criticize) the art you see.

✦ 224 ✦

"BAREFOOT IN THE PARK"
A great movie and a great idea. Find a park
you haven't visited lately. Hold hands, look at the flowers,
spot the animals, and, of course, take off your shoes.

✦ 225 ✦

THE NEXT SUPERSTAR
Go on a talent search for the best local talent
in your area. Visit all the live music spots you can find.

✦ 226 ✦

MATCHMAKERS
Set two of your friends up on a date. Now, you
and your Love spy on them while they're out. Call each one
the next day to hear what they thought of the date.

❧ 227 ❧

3-D DATE
Do drinks, dinner, and dancing.

❧ 228 ❧

URBAN COWBOYS
...or not, attend a rodeo together.
Don't forget to dress appropriately.

❧ 229 ❧

READY, AIM, FIRE
Spend an afternoon together at a firing
range perfecting your marksmanship skills.

❧ 230 ❧

CALLER I.D.
Use those well-honed phone skills and work
on a telethon or "get out the vote" phone bank together.

✦ 231 ✦

HOLY SMOKES

Warning: This is a radical, wild, spontaneous date, not to be
tried by everyone. Find a place that does body piercing, and
both have something pierced on your bodies.

✦ 232 ✦

IT'S A PUZZLEMENT

Find a 1,000-piece puzzle and agree the two of you will put it
together in one day.

✦ 233 ✦

A, B_{12}, C

Find a vitamin store and investigate
which vitamins the two of you should be taking.
Then, remind each other to take them.

✦ 234 ✦

FRUITS & VEGETABLES

Locate a farmer's market or a special place where they sell produce and select the best fruits and vegetables together.

✦ 235 ✦

DATED MOVIE

Locate the movie that won the Academy Award in the year of your birth and watch it together.

✦ 236 ✦

BUMP IN THE NIGHT

Have a battle of the bumper cars
with your Love one evening.

✦ 237 ✦

FAT-FREE

In fact, this date is calorie-free as well.
Agree to spend a quiet day together fasting.

✦ 238 ✦

AN ACT OF SHARING
Take Communion. The two of you can do it together, or you can receive the sacrament at most Christian churches.

✦ 239 ✦

STORM WARNING
Sit down with your Love and have a brainstorming session on ways to improve your relationship. Remember, no idea is a bad one, and you must keep an open mind.

✦ 240 ✦

AMATEUR GOURMET
Browse a gourmet store together. Each select and taste foods neither of you have eaten before.

✦ 241 ✦

TONGUE-TIED
Find out which one of you is better with tongue twisters.

✦ 242 ✦

TAKE A STAND
Together, write a letter to your paper's editor about an
article with which the two of you strongly agreed or disagreed.

✦ 243 ✦

TEST DRIVERS
Spend the afternoon test driving cars you can't afford.

✦ 244 ✦

THREE'S A CROWD
Not when it's a good friend. Invite a single friend to join the
two of you for dinner.

✦ 245 ✦

HOP ALONG
When was the last time the two of you went
bar-hopping together? Try to get to five bars in one evening.

✦ 246 ✦

SEARCH FOR THE WORD
Find out the sermon topics at the
churches and/or temples in your area, then pick one and go.
Afterward, discuss the sermon over brunch.

✦ 247 ✦

MEMORIAL PARK
Cemeteries should be thought of as beautifully kept
parks full of interesting spirits. Spend an afternoon walking
around the grounds. Pick your favorite epitaph.

✦ 248 ✦

NO MORE HANGUPS
Help each other hang up all those pictures
that have been laying on the floor around the house.

✦ 249 ✦

A SHOT AT STARDOM
The two of you audition for parts
in a local play or as extras on a movie set.

✦ 250 ✦

9 TO 5
Tell each other tales about all your co-workers.

✦ 251 ✦

A DASH OF NEW ORLEANS
Both of you dressup as if you are
going to Mardi Gras. Dine on Cajun food.

✦ 252 ✦

BLUE GENES
Any noble blue-blood running through
your veins? Find out. Spend the day together tracing
the genealogy of your family tree.

❖ 253 ❖

DREAM HOME

Have fun looking at furniture. Fantasize about the
kind of furniture you would choose for your dream home

❖ 254 ❖

NOT SO BAZAAR

Find a church bazaar in your area and hunt
for some homemade goodies and handicrafts.

❖ 255 ❖

GETTING IN THE SWING

Take a golf lesson together.

❖ 256 ❖

GIVE A HAND

Learn about yourselves from a handwriting analyst. For fun,
try crossing your "I's" and dotting your "T's."

❖ 257 ❖

GAME SHOWS

Tune into "Jeopardy," "Wheel of Fortune," or any
other game show and play along together. Keep score,
including a score on Vanna's outfit.

❖ 258 ❖

GO PUBLIC

Spend a quiet afternoon together in
the public library. Steal a kiss between the stacks.

❖ 259 ❖

MEMORABLE MEMORIAL

Celebrate your own Memorial Day together
by laying wreaths on the graves of you and your partner's
loved ones. Share fond memories about
those people with each other.

✦ 260 ✦

JUNK RUN

Make a late-night junk food run together.

✦ 261 ✦

UP, UP, AND AWAY

Have fun filling a bunch of balloons with helium and then setting them free. See how many people come around to see what's being celebrated.

✦ 262 ✦

FAN-TO-FAN

Write to a favorite celebrity of both of yours. Ask for an autographed picture and membership in their fan club.

✦ 263 ✦

POP TOP

Rent a convertible and drive it with the top down.

✦ 264 ✦

SCHEME TEAM

Team up together to plan and execute an elaborate practical joke on a good-natured friend.

✦ 265 ✦

GOLDEN SENIORS

Spend the afternoon visiting your grandparents or someone elderly in a senior citizens home. You'll find they really are national treasures.

✦ 266 ✦

WHAT DAY IS IT?

Well, it's whatever special holiday the two of you decide. So celebrate. Come up with some crazy traditions and decorations. If you had fun, mark your calendars for next year.

✦ 267 ✦

PRE-DATE DATE

Sit down and select the dates you both like best
out of this book. Then, schedule them on your calendars.

✦ 268 ✦

PROM KING & QUEEN

Recreate your prom or create the prom
you never had with your Love. Drag out those old clothes or
improvise. Buy matching corsages and boutonnieres.
Dance to music from that year.

✦ 269 ✦

TAXI PICKUP

Send a taxi to pick up your Love after work. Give the
cab driver instructions to a special restaurant and be waiting
outside when your Love's cab pulls up.

✦ 270 ✦

PERSONAL STARDOM

Buy a star for your Love through the Ministry
of Federal Star Registration at 1-800-528-STAR. When you
receive the certificate listing the coordinates of your Love's
star, spend an evening stargazing until you find it.

✦ 271 ✦

ROYALTY FOR A DAY

Spend the day calling each other "Your Highness"
and "Your Majesty." If you want to go a little farther, wear
crowns and carry royal scepters.

✦ 272 ✦

WINDOW WONDERLAND

Together, choose your favorite herbs for a kitchen-window
herb garden. Shop for seeds or small plants, plant them
together, and watch them grow.

✦ 273 ✦

I SPY

Agree to go shopping, but one of you is to be a detective, and the other a suspect. See if the detective can stay out-of-sight until the suspect returns to the car.

✦ 274 ✦

MAD HATTER

Pick out hats for each other to wear to dinner. Keep them on the whole evening and enjoy the reactions from people.

✦ 275 ✦

SURPRISE, SURPRISE

Surprise your Love with a surprise party for no particular reason.

✦ 276 ✦

TATTOO YOU

Visit a tattoo parlor and pretend to be shopping for tattoos for the two of you. Who knows, maybe you will get one.

❖ 277 ❖

'B'—₁ AS IN BOY— 6

Find a bingo hall and go play bingo together.

❖ 278 ❖

CAMP IN

Pitch a pup tent in your living room. If you don't have a tent,
a makeshift sheet will do the trick. Eat on the floor in front
of the fireplace, then snuggle in for the evening.

❖ 279 ❖

JUST A QUIZ

Most churches offer relationship quizzes in their premarital
classes. Take the quiz for fun. Remember, it's just a quiz.

❖ 280 ❖

WE'RE ALL ADULTS

Therefore, find, select, sign up,
and go to an adult education class together.

✦ 281 ✦

FANCY FEET

It can be country, ballroom, or belly, sign up for a dance class
together and try it at least once.

✦ 282 ✦

TAKE A HIKE

Locate a beautiful location to take
a nice long hike. Wear comfortable shoes, bring water,
and chat through the wilderness together.

✦ 283 ✦

TURTLENECKING

Find out where the local hangout is for
necking and go. Bring music, blanket, food, and Chapstick
(let's hope you'll need it afterward).

❧ 284 ❧

SOAP GETS IN YOUR EYES
Find a store with a large selection of soaps and,
together, pick out soaps you both like. Then, go home
and test out your favorites on each other.

❧ 285 ❧

SCENT-SATIONAL
Don't guess which fragrance your Love likes best,
spend the afternoon shopping together for the perfect per-
fume or cologne for each other.

❧ 286 ❧

CRASH & BURN
Go ice skating together. Perhaps you might
want to bring a pillow and belt it around your crash site.

❧ 287 ❧

HOTEL HOP
Make a date to visit several hotels in one night.
Stop for coffee or a drink in each. Then, ask to see a sample
room or suite at each spot. Tell them you're considering
booking a romantic weekend.

❧ 288 ❧

MASTERS' MASTERPIECES
Check for a touring exhibit or just choose
a museum the two of you haven't visited recently. Spend time
exploring and discussing the works.

❧ 289 ❧

GET DOWN & DIRTY
Visit a local greenhouse and wander
among the flora, together. Choose a plant the two of you
feel represents your Love and bring it home to plant
together. Gloves optional.

✦ 290 ✦

RUBBER DUCKY RACE
Pack for a picnic by a stream and include
two rubber duckys. Upstream, place the duckys in the water,
then find a nice location downstream to enjoy
the picnic. Be on the lookout for the winning ducky.

✦ 291 ✦

TOYS 'R' YOU
At a toy store together, each pick a toy you
think your Love would like to play with. Now, go home and
play with your toys. Don't forget to share.

✦ 292 ✦

EVERYTHING YOU LEARNED IN KINDERGARTEN
Finger-paint, show & tell, listen to a story,
have a cookie and juice break, then nap.

✦ 293 ✦

SIMON SAYS

Play Simon Says together. Be fair and alternate being Simon.

✦ 294 ✦

OPEN WIDE

Dinner tonight must be fed to you by your Love and vice versa. Teamwork is required, and remember to open wide.

✦ 295 ✦

TUNE IN

Go to a music store and each pick out music from a new artist, then go home and listen together.

✦ 296 ✦

BEDTIME TALE

Go to bed early and read a bedtime story to your Love. If all goes well, you may want to make this a ritual until the book is finished.

❖ 297 ❖

GAMESMANSHIP
Pick a game Twister, Monopoly, strip poker, or whatever.
Enjoy competing against your Love.

❖ 298 ❖

THE UN-BIRTHDAY
Trying to throw your Love a surprise birthday party? Throw
that party a month (or even months) early or late.

❖ 299 ❖

SUBJECTIVE THINKING
Think of a subject the two of you have always wanted to
know more about such as Egyptian antiques, the mating
habits of ants, or edible plants. Research the subject together.
Go to the library or pick up a phone book and call experts.
Don't stop till you have your questions answered.

✦ 300 ✦

DRIVE-IN SURPRISE
Go to your favorite drive-in restaurants and buy your favorite
food item from each one. Have a picnic.

✦ 301 ✦

CAR WASH HAPPENING
Wash your cars together, with both washing the same car at
the same time.

✦ 302 ✦

FILL IN THE BLANKS
Each of you write a list of sentences
you want your Love to finish. Let your Love fill in the
blanks, then review your Love's responses. Lively
conversation is guaranteed. Some examples: I Love you
because___. You make me laugh when you___.
My favorite outfit on you is___.

✦ 303 ✦

MYSTIC PIZZA
Find a fortune teller, palmist or tarot card
reader for the two of you to go visit. Enjoy listening to what
they say, then discuss the results over a pizza.

✦ 304 ✦

MR. M.D.
Play doctor. Agree on the
type of doctor first. Don't forget to take turns.

✦ 305 ✦

PERSONAL ARTIFACTS
Together gather up all those meaningful
things around the house that have no special place, and put
them into a beautiful box for the two of you to enjoy going
through from time to time.

✦ 306 ✦

CLOSET ENCOUNTERS
Plan to have a romantic dinner together in one of your closets.

✦ 307 ✦

DINNER WHERE?
Plan to have dinner in an unusual place
in your home. Some suggestions are the guest room, the base-
ment, the attic, the shower, the bathtub.

✦ 308 ✦

ROLODEX ROULETTE
Sit down with your Love and make a list of favorite
restaurants and stores with their telephone numbers.
Now the two of you have the perfect reference for
gifts and special occasions. Agree to keep it current
and in an easily accessible place.

✦ 309 ✦

THE FIRST TIME
Remember the first date you had together? Well, try to
recreate it. If possible, see if you can dress and look the same.

✦ 310 ✦

PRETTY FEET
Feet have got to be the most unattractive part of our bodies.
Pretty up your Love's feet with a personal pedicure.

✦ 311 ✦

TICKETS TO PARADISE
Buy two tickets to a concert, play,
sporting event, or movie that your Love wants to see.

✦ 312 ✦

TEN GROOMED DIGITS
Personally manicure your Love's hands. You might
get lucky, and the favor will be returned.

✦ 313 ✦

FASHION PARADE

Make appetizers and drinks for your Love.
While your partner is sitting in a comfortable chair
eating and enjoying the atmosphere, model all the outfits
you're considering throwing out of your closet, and let your
Love help you make the final decision.

✦ 314 ✦

SURPRISE EVENING

Announce to your Love that you are surprising him or her with
a special dinner. Have his or her clothes laid out, paste on his
or her toothbrush, fragrance at the ready, and bath drawn.
Then, you're off. Oh, don't forget to make a reservation.

✦ 315 ✦

WEEKEND BREAKFAST

Get up early one weekend morning and make breakfast for
the two of you. Serve your Love breakfast in bed. Remember
the morning paper and don't forget to clean up after yourself.

✦ 316 ✦

NO PEEKING

Blindfold your Love and take them to a surprise evening.
Some suggestions: movie, dinner, picnic, or concert. Note:
make sure your Love is dressed appropriately.

✦ 317 ✦

BACK SCRATCH FEVER

Treat your Love to a great back scratch. Don't have
the fingernails for it? Try a hair brush or loofah sponge, if you
don't have a back scratcher.

✦ 318 ✦

GO FISH

Literally. Collect all the gear, choose a spot or rent a boat,
pack a lunch, and go fishing together. It really is fun with
someone you love.

✦ 319 ✦

IT'S A STRIKE
Go bowling together.

✦ 320 ✦

HEAD STRONG
Spend the evening on each other's head. Massage
your Love's scalp, shampoo and condition his or her hair,
then blow and brush your Love's locks dry.

✦ 321 ✦

COOKIE FACTORY
Turn your kitchen into a cookie factory and
make cookies for the people you care about. Wrap them in
special paper —if they are going to loved ones
out-of-town. Hand deliver the ones to be given to nearby
friends. For fun, you could ring the door bell, then run.

❧ 322 ❧

DOWN MEMORY LANE

Gather up all the photos laying around. Now,
go through them with your Love. Write everything the two of
you can remember on the back. If you can, try and
organize the photos chronologically.

❧ 323 ❧

A COLORFUL TIME

Buy two coloring books and enjoy filling them
in together. Remember to share your crayons or magic mark-
ers, and it's okay to draw outside the lines.

❧ 324 ❧

DOUBLE BUBBLE

A bubble bath for two is a tried and
true winner. So do it. Get out the candles, turn on the music,
wash the strawberries, pop the champagne, fluff up
the towels, turn off the lights, select the soaps, and draw the
bath. Hey, go ahead and even float a rubber ducky.

✦ 325 ✦

KISS MARKS THE SPOT
Find out what spots on your Love are their most pleasing to have touched. Do this by giving them a full body massage and promising to kiss every spot they point out. Ask for feedback on how they like that spot touched.

✦ 326 ✦

CARTING AROUND
Go for a drive around a golf course on a golf cart. Many public golf courses will allow you to rent just the cart. However, please make sure to observe the course's cart etiquette.

✦ 327 ✦

BUCK FREE
Spend an afternoon handing out ten or more $1 bills randomly to people for no reason other than their reaction.

❧ 328 ❧

CECIL B. DEMILLE

Find or borrow a video camera. Find a public spot
and interview strangers for an alleged documentary. Think
up ridiculous questions to ask like: "What is your
opinion on soap?" or "Who would be the best child
President?" Afterward, order take-out,
then go home and watch your new video.

❧ 329 ❧

IT'S IN THE WATER

Eat a watermelon together and
see who can spit the seeds the farthest.

❧ 330 ❧

CITY TOUR

Rent a cab or board a tour bus and pretend
you're from out-of-town and want a tour. Enjoy the new
and laugh at the baloney.

✦ 331 ✦

REARRANGEMENT
Pick a room, rearrange it together to give it a new look.

✦ 332 ✦

SHAMPOO YOU
Wash, condition, and blow dry your
Love's hair. Then, hint around about receprocating.

✦ 333 ✦

FAN THE FLAME
Think of someone the two of you
really like and write them a fan letter.

✦ 334 ✦

NOSE-TO-NOSE
Lie together side-by-side touching noses and
share the events of the day. A benefit to this position is an
increased probability of getting kissed.

✦ 335 ✦

DREAM CAR

Go shopping for your dream car in the dealer's parking lot at
night after the dealership is closed.

✦ 336 ✦

FOR THE BIRDS

Buy a bird-watchers guide, and see how many birds in your
area you can identify.

✦ 337 ✦

CELESTIAL BODY

On a clear night, get out an astrological map and together try
to find your zodiac signs in the stars.

✦ 338 ✦

WATER DOWN

Draw your water balloons, squirt guns, sprinklers, hoses, or
whatever. Choose your weapons and prepare to get wet.

❧ 339 ❧

SPARE CHANGE

Grab your spare change, then find some
public place where the two of you will have a good view.
Now, throw out change onto the ground and watch
people's reactions. Get bold and try a buck, but stand back.

❧ 340 ❧

FLY A KITE

When was the last time you did? Buy one
that the two of you have to assemble or make one
of your own. Now, go fly a kite.

❧ 341 ❧

CUT & PASTE

Agree on someone you'd like to send a special letter. Collect
all your old magazines, and cut and paste together a letter to
send. If you want, your message may be anonymous.

✦ 342 ✦

BUBBLES
Buy two bubble blowing kits and have a
bubble blowing competition.

✦ 343 ✦

RODIN WITH A POP
Buy a variety of balloon shapes and see which one of you can
make the most interesting balloon sculpture.

✦ 344 ✦

WHITTLIN' AWAY THE DAY
Find two pocket knives, two pieces of wood, and a back
porch and whittle away. Rocking chairs optional.

✦ 345 ✦

TOUCHED BY A NEWBORN
Many hospitals need volunteers to feed newborns in their
nursery. Spend an evening helping others and yourselves.

❧ 346 ❧
MORE S'MORE
In the fireplace or over a fire outside, have all
the fixins' ready to make s'mores (toasted marshmallows,
chocolate squares, graham crackers). Can't find
a fire? Turn off the lights in the kitchen and toast your
marshmallows over your electric or gas range.

·

❧ 347 ❧
HOT HORS D'OEUVERS
Buy an inexpensive hibachi and take it to a
remote spot outside where the two of you can spend a happy
hour (or two) drinking and eating hot
hors d'oeuvers together.

❧ 348 ❧
DON'T SPIT IT OUT
You each chew a wad of bubble gum, then compete
for the biggest bubble. Explosion maintenance is critical.

✦ 349 ✦

LAWRENCE WELK EFFECT
Blow bubbles out a window or from behind a wall and watch
the effect it has on people and animals.

✦ 350 ✦

IN THE CARDS
Everyone has personal business cards. Why not couple cards?
Design and print some for the two of you to hand out to cou-
ples you like. Include both of your phone numbers.

✦ 351 ✦

FAST-FOOD CONTEST
Find a fast-food restaurant and sit where
you can watch the people coming in and the pickup line.
Now, the two of you guess what a person is going
to order, then check your guess when they collect their food.

✦ 352 ✦

PARTY CRASHER
For the bold at heart. Dress up and find
a party to crash. Mingle with the guests and dance to the
band. However, don't eat or drink unless its a
cash bar. It's not right that the host has to pick up your tab.

✦ 353 ✦

A DIFFERENT LIGHT
Spend an evening in candlelight. Put candles
on the dinner table, in the bathroom, in the bedroom...every-
where. The romance bug will definitely bite.

✦ 354 ✦

THE PERFECT PILLOW
Isn't it time you changed the pillows you've been
sleeping on? There are so many new kinds to choose from
now. Go pillow shopping and enjoy the rewards tonight.

✦ 355 ✦

JUICY FRUIT

Make homemade juices together. Select some fruits that you
both like, take them home, and squeeze away.

✦ 356 ✦

IT'S A JOKE

Everyone wishes they had a bigger collection of jokes to tell.
Spend some time together going through joke books and
calling friends to increase each person's repertoire.

✦ 357 ✦

TIRED OF BEING TIRED

Take a nap together while holding hands.

✦ 358 ✦

COAT OF ARMS

Find or design a coat of arms that represents your relationship.
You can then print it on stationery, linens, T-shirts, etc.

✦ 359 ✦

CLEAN, CLEANER, CLEANERS

Chances are each of you uses a different dry cleaner. Spend an afternoon shopping for a dry cleaner's that you can share. Talk to the owner or manager. Does either owner voluntarily resew loose buttons? Clean stark-white items?

✦ 360 ✦

THE LANGUAGE OF LOVE

Take a class together in one of the romance languages—like French. Once you've learned the language, spend a weekend creating the atmosphere of the country, eating the food, and speaking the language.

✦ 361 ✦

TIP TOP TOPLESS

Together, visit an "adult entertainment" spot, but instead of watching the show—watch the audience!

✦ 362 ✦

READING IS FUNDAMENTAL
Select a book you both want to read and take turns reading it
to one another.

✦ 363 ✦

GOOD BUSINESS
Spend the day together organizing your Love's office space.

✦ 364 ✦

THE RANCH
Go on a trail ride together or with a local group. Rent a horse
and see who can ride the best—or at least stay on the horse.

✦ 365 ✦

THE ROMANCE OF CANOEING
Many places offer old-fashioned midnight
canoe rides for couples. Afterwards, cozy up to an
outdoor fire and roast some marshmallows.